CITY POEMS

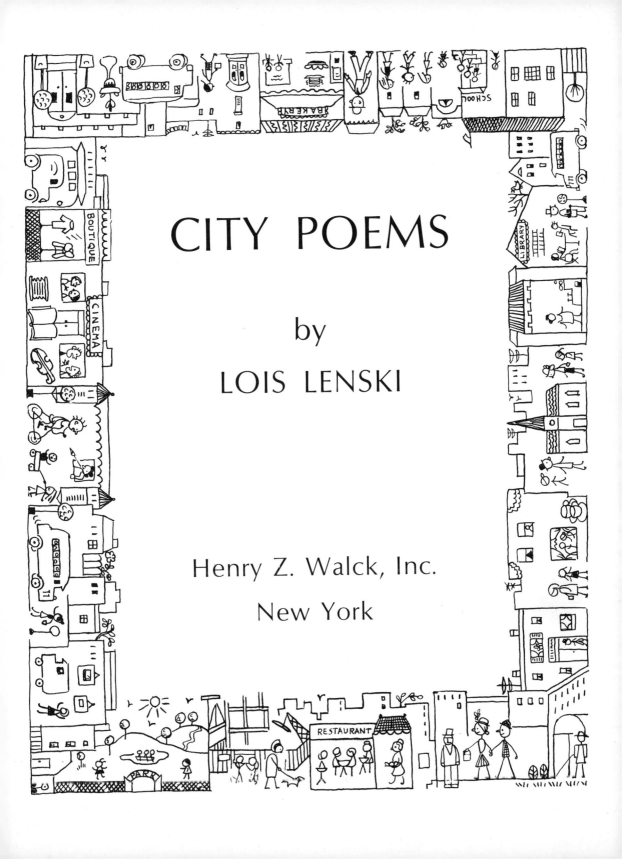

CITY POEMS

by

LOIS LENSKI

Henry Z. Walck, Inc.

New York

```
811      Lenski, Lois
  L         City poems.   Walck, 1971
            128p.   illus.

            Includes index of titles and first
         lines.
            Poems, mostly new, about people,
         places, homes, and fun in the city.



         1. Cities and towns - Poetry   I. Title
```

This Main Entry catalog card may be reproduced without permission.

Copyright 1954, 1965 by Lois Lenski; © copyright 1956, 1971 by Lois Lenski. All rights reserved. ISBN: 0-8098-2414-0. Library of Congress Catalog Card Number: 70-119569. Printed in the United States of America.

CONTENTS

FOREWORD

Over twenty years ago, Lois Lenski had the courage and foresight to write books for children about the slums and about poverty in our cities and country. Hers was one of the first voices in children's literature to "tell it like it is," portraying such authentic characters as drunken fathers, improvident parents, and vicious neighbors as part of the everyday life of the urban and rural child.

Lois Lenski's Roundabout America Series and her American Regional Series represented a breakthrough in the literature that idealized childhood, to that which portrayed real children facing real problems. Facts were not sugarcoated, settings were vividly described, solutions to problems were not over-simplified, and endings, while hopeful, were not always happy.

Interspersed in many of Miss Lenski's books for children were poems and songs. These were all gathered together for the first time in a collection titled *The Life I Live*. Now, in this volume, *City Poems*, Lois Lenski has brought together over ninety new verses and some twenty-five previously published ones to make a collection of city poems for young children.

Unlike much of today's poetry of protest that is filled with hatred and despair, Miss Lenski's verse reflects the point of view of children who respond to the excitement and events of city living. Having no point of comparison, the young child does not think of his house as sordid or ugly, but as home. He sees beauty in the colors and rhythm of the blinking "City Lights" and in a "Flower So Red," the titles of two of Miss Lenski's poems.

It is the nature of the child to make his own fun wherever he can and with whatever is available. This characteristic is reflected in the verses "Hideout" and "Street Closed." The arrival of "Spring in the City" may be celebrated in such traditional ways as playing hopscotch or flying a kite, or defiantly kicking garbage cans down the street.

The city child meets many people in his daily life and they are all here in Lois Lenski's verses: the zoo-keeper, the newsboy, the shoeshine boy, the mailman, the doctor, and the ice cream man. Hordes of nameless people also rush through these poems, creating the helpless feeling of anonymity. This dehumanization process begins early and is reflected in the lines: "Sing a song of people / Who like to come and go: / Sing of city people / You see but never know!"

While the child in these poems can see some beauty and joy in the city, he also knows loneliness and fear, genuine emotions of childhood. The stark narrative poem "Accident" communicates fear, pain, and overwhelming relief as the hurt child's mother arrives at the hospital. Inability to pay the rent and fear of being thrown out on the streets is the theme of the poem "Rent Man." The violence of gangs and the terror of riots are a part of the daily experience of city children and so poems of each of these appear in this collection.

Once again Miss Lenski has provided children with authentic and appropriate content. She has not ascribed to children such adult emotions as bitterness, sarcasm or cynicism, but neither has she glossed over such universal emotions as loneliness, fear, or anger. She has consistently seen with the eyes of the child, reflecting beauty and joy in the midst of ugliness. She has heard the rhythms of the city through his ears, and she has felt the pain and loneliness of the city child today. Characteristically, Lois Lenski's last poem in the book is titled "Star in the Sky." Filled with complaints of city living, the final verse of this poem ends on a hopeful note: "Ain't no daylight / Clothes won't dry: / But sometimes at night / A star in the sky." The literature of despair is not for children, but the literature of honest realism is. In all her writing, both poetry and prose, Lois Lenski has been honest with children and hopeful for them.

Charlotte S. Huck, *Professor of Education*
The Ohio State University

PREFACE

Although I grew up in a small town and have written many stories of small town and rural life, I have always been in love with the city. When I first came to New York many years ago as an art student, I developed the sketch-book habit and spent much of my spare time sketching in the pushcart section of the Lower East Side. I was fascinated by the teeming multitudes of people, their activities, interests and dialects. Some of my sketches were later developed into oil paintings, one of which was hung, to my great pride and satisfaction, in the National Academy of Design exhibition.

City life has always appealed to artists and writers. Where else can one find so much lively subject matter in such close compass? Here is an unending panorama of human life presented, as on a stage, for the benefit of the discerning onlooker. The writer, and especially the poet, wants to delve into hidden motives and meanings—to really enter the people's lives, so that he can interpret them with understanding. My stories of city life, based on experiences with actual city people, have been a great joy to write.

City life lends itself particularly well to poetic expression, and poetry for children, which should not necessarily be dependent upon form or technique, must say something. It must communicate, it must have meaning for the child reader. Poetic expression uses words to convey an impression or a feeling, to interpret actions and even to tell a story— but always with artistry and restraint, which give accent to meaning and poignancy. A poem for children should illuminate the subject, as prose cannot do, by its selection of well-chosen words, thereby conveying the essence of a way of life. The writer should be greatly moved by his subject, and if he is, he may be sure that the poem will, in turn, greatly move his readers.

City life, such an unending panorama, offers color, variety, form and pattern. It offers drama and conflict of individuals and groups, and a continuous pageant of human emotions displayed by all. I hope that my love for the city is reflected in the poems in this book, so that those who have never lived in the city may have the vicarious experience of sharing its joys and sorrows with those who do, with those to whom it is a chosen or necessary way of life.

Lois Lenski

I LIKE THE CITY

IN THE CITY

The buildings are tall,
The people are small—
                    In the city.

The noises are loud,
There's always a crowd—
                    In the city.

The cars move fast,
Great trucks jolt past—
                    In the city.

Up in the sky
The pigeons fly—
                    In the city.

East or west,
I like it best—
                    In the city.

WHAT IS A CITY?

A city is a place laid out
    In blocks, with streets between;
Where cars and trucks go in and out
    And busy crowds are seen.

A city is a place made of
    Tall buildings in a row;
With churches, banks and offices,
    And schools where children go.

A city is a place with room
    For theaters with lights;
Cafes and restaurants and stores,
    And strange, unusual sights.

A city is a place with homes
    Where many people live;
They come and go, they buy and sell,
    They love and hate and give.

A city is a place made up
    Of concrete, steel and stone;
Though it is hard and oft unkind,
    To millions it is home.

3

CITY STREET

Honk—honk—honk!
Beep—beep—beep!
　Hear the noise
　Of city street.

Cars race fast,
Trucks bump past;
Creeping slow
The buses go.

Green turns red,
A sudden stop;
Up the hand
Of traffic cop.

Whistle shrill—
All is still;
Sudden hush—
The people rush.

Red turns green,
Then on again;
Cars race fast,
Trucks bump past.

DON'T CROSS THE STREET

Don't cross the street,
　Wait for a light;
When it turns green,
　That's all right.

Don't cross the street
　When the light is red;
A truck will hit you
　And kill you dead.

Look to the left
　And look to the right;
You only cross over
　On a green light.

I LOVE THE CITY

I love the life of the city,
    Where there's never a dull minute;
There's always something happening,
    And when it does, you're in it.

I love the speed of the city,
    Where things move very fast;
Trucks and taxis, people—
    If you don't hurry, you'll be last!

I love the crowds of the city,
    Where all the people rush;
They're all in a hurry to get there,
    If you can't keep up—just push!

RAIN IN THE CITY

The warm sun gone now,
Cold the rain blows;
Heat of summer forgotten,
Mist comes and goes.

Coats out of storage now,
Collars turned up high;
Umbrellas bending
Under rain from the sky.

Comes a gale of wind
Down a passageway;
Umbrella inside out—
Throw it away.

Walk through the streets now,
Like a blind man led;
Creeping and crawling,
Go home to bed.

MY HEART IS IN THE CITY

My heart is in the city—
    Oh, how I like to be
One of the millions stepping
    Along the street so free!

My heart is in the city,
    I love it all so well—
Its streets, its parks, its people,
    Its pleasures all I tell.

My heart is in the city—
    What fun it is to ride
An airplane up to witness
    Its streets spread far and wide.

My heart is in the city—
    Oh, what a lovely sight
To see the giant buildings
    All lighted up at night!

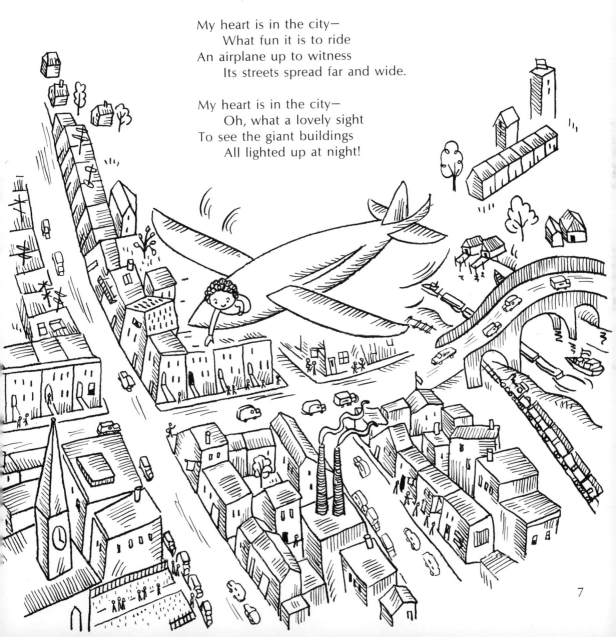

APARTMENT HOUSE

The doorman stands beside the door
    Under a canopy green;
He wears the smartest uniform—
    He always makes sure to be seen.

A lady comes out of the apartment house,
    Taking her dog for a walk;
She tilts her nose up in the air
    And never stops to talk.

Old man toddles out on uncertain feet,
    And hails a cab for a ride;
The doorman opens up the door,
    And helps the old man inside.

The doorman goes back to his place
    Under the canopy green;
He stands and watches the traffic go by—
    He always makes sure to be seen.

PENTHOUSE

Up on the penthouse roof
We can look down far below—
Down to the streets and see
Where many people go.

Up on the penthouse roof
We can look off far away—
Away to the river blue,
Where boats sail by all day.

Up on the penthouse roof
We can look up to the sky—
Up to the white, white clouds
Where birds and airplanes fly.

Up on the roof by day
We are close to sky and sun;
Close to the moon and stars
At night when day is done.

BIRTHDAY CAKE

The birthday cake was beautiful,
　　With frosting pink and blue;
He packed it up so carefully
　　And handed it to you.

You could not wait to take it home,
　　You hurried from the shop;
You tried to cross the busy street,
　　You stumbled, let it drop.

Policeman came and picked you up,
　　A boy picked up the cake;
You took it, then he called a cab,
　　A cab for you to take.

The birthday cake was beautiful,
　　Though mashed and crumpled some;
All the party children ate,
　　Left not a single crumb!

LET'S RIDE THE BUS

Bus stop at the corner,
Just stand right there and wait;
Here it comes, door opens,
Hop in and don't be late.

Hop in, hop out!
Hear the driver shout.
There's room for more
Don't block the door.
Hop in, hop out!

Have your money ready,
Just drop it in the slot;
Find a seat that's empty,
Or stand up like as not.

Bus starts up. It's going!
It can't go very fast.
All the trucks and autos
And taxis going past.

Now it's going faster,
You'd better hang on tight;
Going round the corner,
Hold on with all your might.

Now its going slower,
It's coming to your stop;
Time to ring the buzzer,
Get up and out you hop!

Hop in, hop out!
Hear the driver shout!
There's room for more,
Don't block the door.
Hop in, hop out!

PEOPLE ON THE BUS

See the people on the bus,
Taking rides just like us.

Bald-headed man, very lame,
Lady with a poodle that is tame.

Giggly girls who smile and smirk,
Mothers coming home from work.

Lady holding bundles on her lap,
Baby with a bottle takes a nap.

Down the aisle a crowd of boys,
Laughing, shouting, making noise.

See the people on the bus,
Taking rides just like us.

AMBULANCE

The siren shrieks
    as speeding fast
The ambulance somber
    goes sailing past.

Carts at the curb
    the people stare;
Through the red lights
    it sails unaware.

Somebody's hurt,
    or very sick;
Speed to the hospital
    quick, quick, quick.

The siren wails
    like a child in pain
Ambulance gone now
    on mission humane.

SHOPPING

I like to go shopping with Mama
    In the big department store;
And ride the escalator
    From the first to the seventh floor.

I like to help Mama buy things,
    Up and down and around we roam;
Then with our arms full of packages,
    We hop on the bus for home.

"Buy the town out?" asks Daddy,
    "No, not quite," we say;
What fun we have opening packages—
    That's the best part of the day!

CITY FIRE

The fire engine comes clanging,
    Roaring down the street;
And all the kids come running,
    With eager pounding feet.

Right around the corner
    The sky is all ablaze;
The siren keeps on screaming,
    The street a smoky haze.

People from the tenements
    Come rushing out to see;
The crowd gets thick and thicker,
    All curious as can be.

A big warehouse is burning,
    The firemen drip, perspire,
Climbing ladders, pouring
    Water on the fire.

At last the fire is over,
    The sky still fiery red;
The engine backs up, clanging,
    And all go home to bed.

ACCIDENT

A boy on a bike
whistles a song;
Car round the corner
plunges headlong.
A crash and a bang,
traffic to a stop;
Boy goes over,
bike on top.
Comes a policeman,
people stare;
Everyone talking,
a siren's blare.

Ambulance comes,
two men in white;
The boy on a stretcher
wrapped up tight.
Away he goes,
safely inside;
As if in a dream,
a speedy ride.
In bed at the hospital,
no one he knows;
Pain in his body
comes and goes.

Sometimes he wakes,
then sleepy again—
Welcome release
from hurt and pain.
Opens his eyes,
someone by the bed;
"He'll soon be OK,"
someone said.
"Who was that?
What did I hear?
Was someone talking—
How did Mom get here?"

GOING TO CHURCH

All dressed up in my Sunday dress,
 A bright red ribbon on my hair;
Clean white socks and shiny new shoes—
 I go tripping down the stair.

All dressed up in my Sunday dress,
 Like most of the people I meet;
I hold up my purse with money inside,
 And go tripping down the street.

All dressed up in my Sunday dress,
 To church I find my way;
I sing a hymn and say a prayer,
 And then feel better all day.

SUNDAY IN THE CITY

The streets are quiet and empty,
 The stores are closed and bare;
Traffic is light and a few people
 Are out walking here and there.

Boys in the street play a ball game,
 As friendly girls call "Hi!"
Old people sit out on benches
 And the day goes slowly by.

Down at the corner a movie,
 A long line leads to the door;
Slowly it moves—all the people
 Vanish inside, rich and poor.

The streets are quiet and empty,
 Over all a Sunday hush;
Few are the cars and the people,
 Silent the week-day rush.

HOMESICK

I'm homesick for the city,
  That's where I belong;
In my crowded building,
  Amid the busy throng.

I never liked the country,
  It is so quiet, still;
I don't like cows or horses,
  I hate each weedy hill;

Out there I saw a bird once,
  Its wings were blue and white;
It never once stopped squawking,
  I could not sleep all night.

Oh, take me to the city,
  Back to its welcome noise;
Back to the kids I play with,
  The city girls and boys.

PLACES IN THE CITY

LANDSCAPE IN CONCRETE

The walls concrete,
The walks the same;
The buildings stone—
A hard cold frame.

The street asphalt,
The girders steel;
Sidewalks harsh
'Neath sole and heel.

A world of stone—
The hardness such,
No softness here
For hand to touch.

No warm response
To impulse tender;
Only callousness
This world can render.

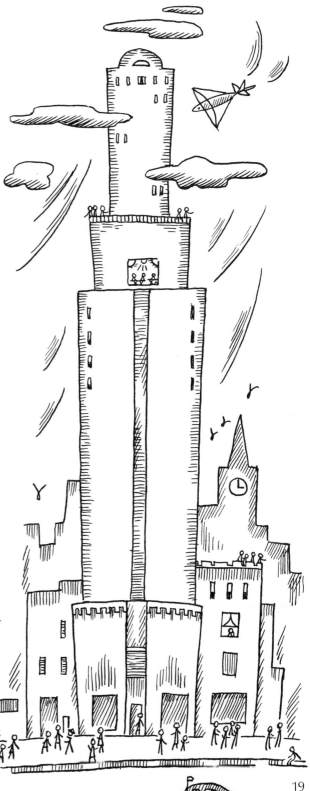

THE SKYSCRAPER

I see a great tall building,
It reaches to the sky;
They call it a skyscraper
And now I can see why.
It has so many windows,
I cannot count them all;
I don't see any chimney,
It stands so high and tall.
It stands there, this skyscraper,
Right on the city street;
And all the city people
Go walking at its feet.
It stands there, this tall building,
So big and tall and high;
Sometimes the clouds it touches—
It almost scrapes the sky!

CITY LIGHTS

The city lights shine
    From dusk till dawn;
Daytime they're off,
    Nighttime they're on.

The city lights shine
    In colors red and blue;
Neon tubes in purple,
    Green and yellow too.

They blaze so bright
All through the night;
    Now off, now on,
    Now off, now on—
Till morning comes
    And night is gone.

A WALK IN THE CITY

A store is at the corner
    for buying milk and butter,
A woman feeds the pigeons
    with grain in the gutter.

Children in the schoolyard
    swinging happily,
Graceful swooping gulls
    fly in from the sea.

Noises of the traffic,
    whistles and a bell,
Busy Teddy's market
    with its fishy smell.

Alley cats come looking
    for meager scraps to eat,
Man with a burden
    stops to rest his feet.

Poultry market busy,
    cackling hens in coops,
Restaurant at the corner,
    smells of hot rich soups.

Sea-going ships at anchor,
    piles of produce hurled,
Soon they will be leaving
    for ports around the world.

FAR-OFF THINGS

As the wind blows sharply
           along the street,
And the trash goes flying
             into the air,
What is it I feel
       as I stop and look,
          Uncertain, standing there?

A softness is in the breeze
That I did not feel before;
The cars are quieter,
         the trucks move so gently
       I don't hear them any more.

What do I feel
          as I stand and wait?
Yes, now I hear it again;
Above the city's loud clamor,
       I hear the voice of spring.

It sings of summer
        and growing things,
Of things the city never knows;
Of far-off things
       in the countryside,
        Of each living thing that grows.

THE PARK

Within the city
Of brick and stone,
A square of green
Grows all alone.

Green of trees
And green of grass,
With winding walks
Where people pass.

Lake of water,
Boats to ride—
Gentle waves
From side to side.

Do not pick
The flowers gay;
On the walks
the children play.

Sloping hills,
Green the grass—
A pretty park
Where people pass.

KEEP OFF

CITY CITY CITY

In the city the houses are close together,
On the streets the stores are tall.
The sidewalks are always full of people—
Does anyone know them all?

All the buses and trucks keep coming and going,
All the cars and taxis too.
But where they go there is no way of knowing,
Or what they intend to do.

Buy dresses in department store,
In shoestore buy your shoes;
At drugstore get your medicine,
To newsstand go for news.

To grocery store you go for food,
To restaurant go to eat;
At candy shop you buy your sweets,
At butcher shop your meat.

In the city the stores are close together,
Along the sidewalks in a row.
People keep coming and people keep going,
But who they are you never know.

CITY MARKET

All night long under dim lights
   The wind blows through the marketplace;
Great trailers unload produce,
   Fill up each inch of space.

Boxes and baskets of fruit,
   Crates of vegetables green,
Grown in all states of the Union,
   In huge piles can be seen.

Pigeons fly down from the rooftop,
   Hunting a seed to peck;
Alley cat slinks through the shadows
   Chewing a chicken neck.

Refuse thrown out by the sellers,
   Rotten potatoes or fruit;
Battered disposal can filling
   With damaged leaf or root.

Boxes and bushels of produce
   Move out to each city stand;
Customers fill up their shopping bags
   And eat of the fruit of the land.

MILK-STAND

The milk-stand at the corner
    Is called an Automat;
You drop the money in the slot,
    And milk comes out like that.

The milk-stand doesn't make it,
    Machines do not know how;
I read a book about it,
    The milk comes from a cow.

A cow out in the country
    Keeps eating grass all day;
The farmer comes and milks it,
    And ships the milk away.

He ships it to the city,
    Where it is bottled up,
And put into the milk-stand—
    I drink it from a cup.

BAKERY SHOP

What do I smell as I go marching
    with a skip and a hippety-hop?
What do I see in the window
    of the shiny new bakery shop?

    Chocolate layer cakes,
    Doughnuts with holes;
    Cookies with nuts,
    Poppyseed rolls.
    Coffee cakes with icing,
    Almond seed cookies,
    Apple and pumpkin pie;
    And a great big wedding cake
        three feet high!

Oh, how I wish I had money
    to buy at the bakery shop!
Off I'd go munching and marching
    with a skip and a hippety hop!

27

LIBRARY

The library is so full of books
    I'd like to read them all;
I think that it would take me
    All winter, spring and fall.

The library is my favorite place,
    I go there everyday;
I put my nose into a book,
    And then I fly away. . . .

Away to other worlds unknown,
    Where I meet people new,
Forget myself, the life I live,
    By living with them too.

The library is so full of books,
    I love them every one;
Each day I keep on going back—
    Book magic is such fun!

CITY SCHOOL

See the children as they come
Down the sidewalk one by one.

Laughing, talking, smiling, gay,
Carrying books to school today.

See the children, large and small,
It is hard to count them all.

Walking, running in the door,
Making room for many more.

Crowded halls with teachers neat,
Children file into each seat.

Now the gong is sure to ring,
That means work will soon begin.

Noisy voices fade away,
No thought now of games to play.

Quiet sounds, a busy hum,
Eager study, work well done.

29

BARBER SHOP

A pole stands at the corner
    With stripes of red and white;
The barber shop is open
    Sometimes till late at night.

The barber is a nice man,
    He hasn't much to say;
He smiles each time he sees you,
    So you won't run away.

A boy can get his hair cut,
    He sits up in the chair;
The lights are bright and blinding,
    He doesn't like the glare.

His hair falls all around him,
    The lotion smells so sweet;
He pays the barber, smiling,
    And goes out in the street.

DELICATESSEN

Gosh! Look at all the food!
The show window is crammed;
And inside—
Shelves, counter and showcases
              are jammed
With all kinds of food.

There's sausage and goat cheese,
Sauerkraut and pig's feet;
Things with funny names
That must be good to eat.
Braunschweiger, limburger,
              pickled beets,
Pumpernickel, liverwurst and
              all kinds of sweets.
Corn beef, ravioli, Chinese chow mein,
Kielbasa, noodles, head-cheese plain;
Bread-and-butter pickles,
              whole-grain bread,
French-fried potatoes and catsup red.
Wienerwurst, herring,
              dill pickles and rye;
Blintzes and bagels—
              don't pass them by.
Get your money out
        from the pockets in your pants,
And don't forget
        the chocolate-covered ants!

Foods with funny names
        must be good to eat;
Delicatessen
        is the place for a treat!

DEPARTMENT STORE

Go in the door
of department store;
See things galore,
then start to buy
and buy some more.

Pants and shirts,
blouses, skirts;
Books and cards,
silk by yards;
Notions, thread,
beads of red;
Pots and pans,
dishes new,
Watches, clocks,
jewelry too.

Escalator up,
hold on tight;
On the top floor,
turn to the right.

Pillowcases, sheet,
shoes for your feet,
Dresses new
in pink and blue
Whatever it is
you need today,
Keep on looking
before you pay.

Escalator down—
don't trip or fall,
Or drop your bundles
large and small
Ended will be
your shopping spree!

Go out the door
of department store;
Take a cab and
come home once more.

THIS WAY
UP

LOIS LENSKI

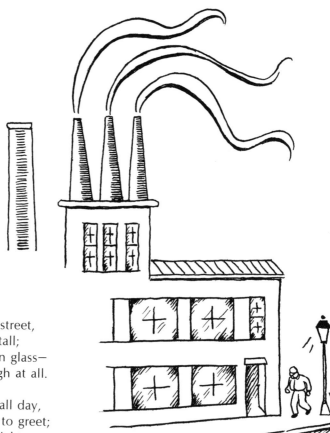

FACTORY

Factory stands on a dingy street,
    Grimy and black and tall;
Windows dirty with broken glass—
    You cannot see through at all.

Factory bangs and bumps all day,
    Loud noises your ears to greet;
All night long the factory lights
    Illumine the dingy street.

Factory men come in, go out,
    Bringing their lunch each day;
Factory man works an eight-hour shift,
    Collects his hard-earned pay.

Factory workers sometimes strike,
    The factory closes down;
The noises stop, the lights go off
    And darken that part of town.

SUPERMARKET

The supermarket is a place
    With food piled very high,
On shelves and counters all around,
    Where people come to buy.

They push a cart and help themselves
    To cookies, meat and pie;
Turnips, pickles, canned goods, bread—
    They fill the cart up high.

Then when they leave, go through a gate,
    A checker checks them through;
They pay their bill, pick up the bags—
    That's all they have to do.

The supermarket is a store
    With every food complete,
Where people pick out what they want,
    And take it home to eat.

35

SUBWAY

Down in the subway under the ground,
The trains keep running all around;
Some go fast and some go slow,
They take you where you want to go.

Under the ground in a tunnel black,
The trains go forward and then come back;
Stop at stations lighted bright,
And take you safely home at night.

Under the streets, the stores, the shops,
The subway train makes many stops.
It's fun to ride on the subway train,
It takes you there and back again.

GHOSTS

The big cranes come
   and knock the walls down;
Bulldozers crawling
   all over the ground.

Stones turn to gravel,
   the bricks to red dust;
Over the earth
   a hard sharp crust.

Above the loud noise
   of creaking crane,
A thin loud wail
   like a creature in pain.

Where is the woman
   in the window calling out?
The children coming home
   with a laugh and a shout?

Where the old man
   on tottery feet?
The people who loved
   this shabby street?

Gone and forgotten—
   but through the dusty air
Their ghosts cry out
   in angry despair.

Gone are their homes,
   No records remain
Of their love or compassion,
   a ghostly refrain.

SUMMER FESTIVAL

In the summer in the city
    There are all kinds of things to do;
Go to concert or museum,
    Or the animals at the zoo.

Take a ride on the rolly-coaster,
    Do square-dancing in the park;
Take the kids to see marionettes
    Or go to the beach for a lark.

In the summer in the city,
    There are all kinds of things to see;
Flowers in bloom at Botanic Gardens,
    Paintings at museums are free.

Fountains are playing in the shopping mall,
    And there's a great big merry-go-round;
Take a ride on a boat on the river,
    And from there watch the sun go down!

PEOPLE IN THE CITY

PEOPLE IN THE CITY

T-shirts, shorts,
Blouses, jeans;
Long hair, short—
Dirty or clean.

Hair-curlers, beards,
Short-sleeves, long;
Bare feet, shoes,
Sandals with thong.

Gay people, sad,
Young people, old;
As many kinds
As the street will hold.

See all the people
Marching along;
Pushing and shoving,
An endless throng.

SPRING IN THE CITY

The wind from the river
    Blows a hat down the street;
A boy with a kite
    Runs on lightning feet.

Little girls turn a rope,
    Chanting a rhyme;
Man at a newstand
    Buys a paper for a dime.

Boys kick a trash can,
    Garbage spills out—
Away they go racing
    With a yell and a shout.

Girls playing hopscotch
    Hop and kick a stone;
Boys start a ball game,
    And leave them alone.

The wind from the river
    Whips the children at play;
A woman hangs up clothes—
    It's spring today.

SING A SONG OF PEOPLE

Sing a song of people
  Walking fast or slow;
People in the city,
  Up and down they go.

        People on the sidewalk,
        People on the bus;
        People passing, passing,
        In back and front of us.
        People on the subway
        Underneath the ground;
        People riding taxis
        Round and round and round.

        People with their hats on,
        Going in the doors;
        People with umbrellas
        When it rains and pours.
        People in tall buildings
        And in stores below;
        Riding elevators
        Up and down they go.

        People walking singly,
        People in a crowd;
        People saying nothing,
        People talking loud.
        People laughing, smiling,
        Grumpy people too;
        People who just hurry
        And never look at you!

            Sing a song of people
                Who like to come and go;
            Sing of city people
                You see but never know!

ELEVATOR BOY

Elevator Boy's Song

Here I go up, up, up,
  Up to the very top;
Right past the doors
  On all the floors,
Until I have to stop.

Here I go down, down, down,
  Dropping down so fast;
Catch your breath,
  It's lots of fun,
I'll get you down at last.

Here I go up, up, up,
  Some get on, then more;
I ask the people,
  "Which floor, please?"
And open up the door.

Here I go down, down, down,
  Down to the street below;
Some get out and some get in,
  Then up again I go!

43

NEWSBOY

Paper! Paper!
Buy a paper, mister!
Read the latest news.

Use your glasses, mister,
Read what's happened, mister,
Keep up with the news.

All about the robbers
And their get-away!
All about the crash-up—
Twenty killed, they say
All about the weather,
Fair and warm today.

Paper! Paper!
Buy a paper, mister!
Read the latest news,
Read the latest news.

POLICEMAN

Policeman wears a uniform,
    He walks along the street;
His job the people to protect
    Within a certain beat.

Policeman represents the law,
    His duty he'll not fail;
Arrests all those who break the law;
    They'll have to go to jail.

Policemen in their uniforms
    Keep order night and day;
Protect the people, enforce the law
    And bravely go their way.

THE MAILMAN

Who is that
in the blue suit and cap?

      The mailman strong
      is marching along.

What's he got there
    on his back?

      A great big pack.
      Letters in envelopes white,
      Letters for people
          who like to write.

Who will get one?

      Neither you nor I
      nor the cat passing by.
      Neither I nor you
      for we never do
      what we're supposed to.

ZOO-KEEPER

What does the zoo-keeper do, do, do?
What does the zoo-keeper do at the zoo?

> I feed the animals every day,
> Give them their meat or their oats or hay;
> And after each meal, sweep the crumbs away—
>   That's what I do at the zoo!

> I let the animals out for air,
> Brush up the hair of the polar bear;
> I chase the monkeys round everywhere—
>   That's what I do at the zoo!

> I throw a fish in the pelican's bill,
> Let all the camels go drink their fill,
> I cover the lion when he takes a chill—
>   That's what I do at the zoo!

> I pat the animals one by one,
> Race them around when they start to run;
> Sometimes I play with them just for fun—
>   That's what I do at the zoo!

What does the zoo-keeper do, do, do?
What does the zoo-keeper do at the zoo?

TAXI DRIVER

I'm a taxi driver,
　　Sitting in my seat!
Watch me drive my taxi
　　Through the city street!

In and out of traffic,
　　Round the city gay—
Bumper hitting bumper,
　　Watch me find my way!

Passenger, just tell me
　　Where you want to go;
I can turn a corner
　　Going fast or slow.

Hurry? sure, I'll hurry!
　　Just sit back and smile;
Hear the meter clicking,
　　Ticking off each mile.

Watch me in my taxi
　　Dodge the crowds so thick;
Don't run over people,
　　Get you there so quick!

See, you're here, I brought you!
　　Pay me what you owe;
Round the great big city
　　Off again I go!

SHOESHINE BOY

Shine, mister, shine?
Shine your shoe
For only a dime?
I'll clean off your shoe,
I'll slick it up fine—
All for a dime.

Look at your shoe!
I'll tap it and slap it
And rap it and strap it.
I'll make it look new
For you,
A shiny new shoe
For you.

I'll make your shoe
Look just like new!
All for a dime,
Shine, mister, shine!

DOCTOR

When I get sick I have to go
To a doctor that I know.

On the elevator to the top.
We get off when it makes a stop.

In his office people wait,
We don't get in till very late.

He feels my pulse, says "Open wide!"
And down my throat he pokes inside.

He feels my forehead—fever too,
He thinks a shot or two will do.

And then I must be very brave,
Of course I know how to behave.

I never scream or cry or bawl—
Pretend it doesn't hurt at all.

But I am glad my Mom came too,
I hear her say, "I'm proud of you!"

ICE CREAM MAN

Tinkle, tinkle, tinkle!
    The ice cream man is coming!
Out from all the houses
    The children all come running.

Chocolate, strawberry, vanilla,
    Which do you prefer?
I'll buy for me a chocolate cone
    And a strawberry one for her.

Tinkle, tinkle, tinkle!
    The ice cream man moves on;
All the cones are dribbling,
    And soon they will be gone.

RENT MAN

Rent man,
Rent man,
Stay away.
Pocket book's empty,
Got no money to pay.

Don't you come round here,
You're not welcome—hear?
This house is our home
All through the year.

Rent man,
Rent man,
Please let us stay.
Don't throw us on the street
Just 'cause we can't pay.
We'll get the money
        next month
Some way . . .
Some way. . . .
Next month we'll pay,
    I say.

LOOK OUT THE WINDOW

I look out the window
Down to the street;
I see the policeman
Walking his beat.
Police car comes,
He hops inside—
Looks like he's going
    Off for a ride.

I look out the window
Down to the street;
Some kids are racing,
With flying feet.
Big trucks honking,
Kids dodge and run;
Newsboy at the corner
    Watches the fun.

Old lady trying
To cross the street;
She's scared of the traffic,
Shaky on her feet;
Newsboy sees her,
Takes her by the arm,
Helps her cross over
    Without any harm.

51

GANG

Like a rushing wind
      the street gang came
Around the corner
      as if playing a game.
Threw stones in windows,
      spilled every trash can,
While onlookers stared,
      then, frightened, ran.

Came the police
      out of nowhere, quick,
All in uniform,
      each with his stick;
The gang disappeared
      like a sudden shower,
The street stayed empty
      for many an hour.

RIOT

Keep off the streets,
  Go home and stay;
Fire alarm's ringing—
  No school today.

Keep children in,
  Comes a loud crash;
Store windows broken,
  Truck in a smash.

Screech goes the siren,
  All the people run;
Bad guys are coming—
  This is no fun.

Curfew at night,
  No time to play;
Keep off the streets,
  Go home and stay.

NDOWS WITH FACES

Windows full of faces
  In the houses on our street;
All the people are my neighbors,
  Though some I never meet.

Old man sits the whole day long,
  Just to pass the time away;
Little boy keeps yelling: "Mom,
  Can I go out on the street and play?"

Man and his wife with angry words,
  Are always in a fight;
They shout and scream as loud as they can
  All through the day and night.

A woman with a dusty mop
  Shakes it out above the street;
Empties her basket of trash
  At passing people's feet.

Little girl sits lonely and sad,
  Watching the street below;
See the children playing
  And cries, too sick to go.

Young man sits and pounds a typewriter,
  Then wipes the sweat away;
Stops to look at a patch of sky,
  And pounds the keys all day.

Landlady with frizzy hair,
  Lets a polite salesman in;
After a noisy argument,
  Out the door he comes again.

Windows full of faces
  Tell of life within;
Laughing, crying, living—
  We are all akin.

FLOWER WAGON

The old brown horse goes plodding,
    Cloppety, cloppety, clop.
His head hangs low and heavy,
    He is always glad to stop.

The peddler calls out, "Flowers!
    Flowers for sale today!"
Geraniums on the wagon
    Are flashing red and gay.

A little boy comes running,
    His money ready to pay;
He buys a pretty flower
    And scampers fast away.

The old brown horse walks slowly,
    Cloppety, clop, and then
The wagon slows the traffic
    Until it stops again.

GOING

Where are the people going?
All the people
    who walk so fast;
Where are they going, going?
I watch them all go past.

Where are they going, the people
Who pass me every day?
They never speak or know me
Or have a word to say.

They seem to be going, going,
But they never take me there;
They're going, going, going—
I wonder where, where, where?

FUN IN THE CITY

PLAYTIME

The sun is shining bright,
It's nice and warm today,
Out in the street we go to play;
We'll join hands,
Dance in a ring,
Listen to us chant and sing!

Hop, skip and jump,
Then down on the pavement,
You fall with a thump.
Go find a ball,
Throw it up against the wall;
Catch it, throw it—
Do not let it fall.

Out in the street we like to play—
Just keep all the cars away.

STREET CLOSED

Street closed
So children can play;
Put up the barriers,
Keep the cars away!

Street closed!
Cars keep out!
Hear the children
Laugh and shout!

PLAY BALL

Stickball, punchball,
All kinds of ball,
But stoopball is the best;
Bounce the ball off the stoop,
Fielder runs to a base
                    and then,
Throw the ball back again.

Boxball, baseball,
Chinese handball too;
Do you know any more?
Let's play them if you do.

MERRY-GO-ROUND

The tent is gay
Ten cents to pay
My horse is bay
Or dapple gray
Hear music play
A roundelay
As round and round
We go—hooray!

Red cheeks aglow
The spring winds blow
We start so slow
Then faster go
Now high now low
We love it so
As round and round
And round we go.

SLIPPERY SLIDE

The slippery slide is very steep,
Up the high ladder you have to creep;
Sit down and take hold
         and give a little push.
Down you go with a swish and a swoosh!
Down you go with a swoosh and a slide,
Down the slippery slide
         you have a quick ride.

Jump off at the bottom,
         around you run,
Up the ladder again
         to have some more fun;
Sit down in your place
         and give a little push—
Down you go with a swish and a swoosh.
Down the slippery, slippery, slippery slide,
Oh, what fun it is to ride!

WHIRLYGIG

The whirlygig whirls around and around,
Step right on it from off the ground;
Push with your foot and step on the side,
It keeps whirling and gives you a ride.

The whirlygig whirls around and around—
Hold on tight or you'll fall to the ground;
Faster and faster it whirls and whirls—
Oh, what fun for boys and girls!

THE SWING

Get on a swing and swing up high,
    As high as you can go;
As high as the stores across the street—
    Then down you come so slow.

Keep on swinging, higher still,
    Until you reach the sky;
Look in somebody's window across the way—
    And wave to a girl going by!

JUNGLE GYM

Come, let's play on the jungle gym,
Climb over our tree from limb to limb;
Crawl in and out and over the top,
Climb up and down without ever a stop;
Climb up and down and all around
Until you get tired and drop to the ground.

On the gym, you're a monkey in the zoo,
You're Tarzan in the jungle climbing too;
Swing hand over hand from left to right,
Grab a banana and pretend to bite;
Climb up to the top and walk on thin air,
The smartest monkey seen anywhere!

AT THE RINK

My leotards red
    and my long tassel cap;
My white leather skating shoes
    buckle with a strap.

My nice new ice skates
    are sharp on the ice;
I totter a minute,
    then off in a trice.

Across the big rink
    I go like a flash;
Long slithery slides,
    then down in a crash.

Across the cold ice,
    I feel like a bird,
On gliding wings
    that float unheard.

BATON

I have my own baton now,
    I love to twirl it gay;
Mom bought me marching records,
    I practice every day.

Up and down and in and out,
    And roundabout I twirl;
Interpreting the music
    With many a fancy swirl.

Marching to the music,
    My pretty costume on,
Everybody looks at me
    Twirling my baton.

SNACK

Give me a sandwich—
  cheese or ham;
Guess you don't know
  how hungry I am.

Give me a hamburger,
  dill pickle too;
Mustard on top—
  that will do.

Plate of French fries,
  catsup red;
Yes, I'm hungry—
  that's what I said!

HIDEOUT

A hideout is a place to play,
A box, a house, a shack.
  You live inside,
  You play inside,
Defend it from attack.

A hideout is a place to wait
For enemies all day;
  You point a gun
  Out just for fun,
And scare them all away.

A hideout is a place to hide
From Indians and from spies.
  You take a peep,
  Around you creep,
And take them by surprise.

HOT DOG HOT

Hot dog hot
And mustard thick,
Watch it sizzle
On a stick.

Hot dog hot,
It smells first rate,
I'm so hungry,
Hate to wait.

Hot dog hot
Inside a roll,
Lots of relish,
Eat it whole.

Oh, how good—
It hits the spot,
Gobble up that
Hot dog hot!

MY NICKEL

Once I had a nickel,
Once I had a dime;
Planned to go and spend 'em
When I had the time.

Want to spend my nickel,
Want to spend my dime;
Buy some sticks of bubble gum
To chew on all the time.

But I lost my nickel,
And I lost my dime;
Pants pocket empty
Now all the time.

Ain't got no nickel,
Ain't got no dime;
Guess I'll be poor now
Rest of the time.

PARADE

A band is playing
    out in the street;
Horns are tooting
    and big drums beat.
A little fife
    plays a merry tune,
    up and down,
    all afternoon.
Behind the band
    the marchers come,
With flags and banners
    and kettle drum.

People line up
    by the curb to see;
They wave their hands
    excitedly;
Windows fly open
    and heads pop out;
People clap hands
    and yell and shout.
Oh, what fun
    to see a parade,
And hear all the music
    the band has made.

THE CHASE

He's chasing me,
I got to run,
Dash round the corner—
This is no fun.

He's coming fast,
My eyes open wide;
I gasp for breath—
Got a pain in my side.

He's coming faster,
A fence I leap,
Stay out of sight
With never a peep.

Then on again
As fast as before;
Up on a roof
And down through a door.

Wild-eyed and panting,
Where shall I go?
I won't let him catch me,
That I know.

Across the street,
Dodge cars and truck;
He's going back—
Boy! What luck!

SHOWER BATH

Heat clamps down,
    Not a breath of air;
Dripping wet
    The few clothes we wear.

Everything's sticky,
    Everything's hot;
Everybody's cross,
    Like as not.

Turn on the hydrant—
    Don't tell the cop;
Give us a sprinkle
    Before we pop!

BENCH IN THE PARK

There's a bench in the park
    At the edge of the walk;
I sit and watch people
    And I hear them talk.

There's only the sidewalk—
    You can't play on the grass;
So I just sit and wait
    For the time to pass.

There's a bench in the park
    Where I sit all day;
A pigeon flies down—
    I shoo it away.

WALKING ON THE SIDEWALK

Walking on the sidewalk,
   I come up to a store;
Sometimes I have to buy things
   And then I walk some more.

Skipping on the sidewalk,
   I don't step on the line;
I hop and skip and jump it,
   So I won't pay a fine.

Playing on the sidewalk,
   Leap-frog, hopscotch hop;
The children all come running,
   We play until we drop.

Skating on the sidewalk,
   I like to skate so fast;
I dodge the crowd of people,
   And skate back home at last.

CHRISTMAS IN THE CITY

Christmas in the city,
See all the stores so bright!
Windows filled with playthings—
    Oh, what a happy sight!

Christmas in the city,
With bells and garlands green;
And Santa at the corner—
    The fattest ever seen!

Christmas in the city—
Oh, what a lot of toys!
Santa says he'll bring them
    To all good girls and boys.

Christmas in the city,
With crowds that push and shove;
They don't seem to remember
    It is a day for love!

71

WINTER COLD

Snow is so deep
       and wet and cold,
Keeps coming down
       fold on fold;
Covers the walks
    and the railroad tracks,
Blows great drifts up
      front and back.

Men with a shovel
      pile it high,
Beside the sidewalk
    where people go by;
Cars get stalled,
     trucks break down,
Too much snow
    in this little old town!

Go get your jacket,
Your rubber boots too;
Zip up your zipper—
Whatever you do.
Let's go out wading,
Make snowballs and throw;
Nothing more fun
Than to play in the snow!

OUR BLOCK IN THE CITY

OUR BLOCK

Our block is a nice one,
   The best in town;
On each side row houses
   With steps coming down.

Our block is noisy,
   We yell and shout—
Women at the windows,
   Children running out.

Our block has music—
   Even a band!
We give a block party,
   It sure is grand!

We hang up flags
   And bunting too;
We dance to the music
   All night through.

We dance till morning,
   And then we rest;
Our block is a nice one—
   The very best.

POKEY OLD MAILMAN

The pokey old mailman
    who brings the mail,
Comes poking along
    through rain or hail.
He pokes along the street
    and stops at each door,
Puts mail in each mailbox,
    and then pokes some more.

The pokey old mailman
    is slow as can be,
He never has letters
    for you or for me;
I never write letters,
    or send them, says he;
That's why, he says daily,
    there's no letter for me.

But once I sent in
    a cereal box-top,
And down it went in
    the mailbox slot.
Our pokey old mailman
    came poking one day,
He brought me a letter—
    hooray! hooray!

NEIGHBOR

A neighbor is a nice lady
    who lives near by;
She comes and baby-sits
    so I won't cry.

She gives me lunch
    when my mother's not home;
She says Mom's gone shopping
    and soon will come.

She has a nice car,
    says she can't be without;
She took me to the hospital
    when I had my tonsils out.

ROSES

Mom has roses,
A pretty bouquet;
They're only plastic—
But I like them, anyway.

In the florist window,
Roses I see;
Maybe they're plastic,
But they look real to me.

When the lady next door
Got sick and died,
Mom went over
And everybody cried.

Somebody sent red roses,
They were so soft to the feel,
I put out my finger to touch them,
And then I knew they were real.

When roses are not real
I can always tell;
Roses are not real
When they have no smell.

I TOOK A WALK

I took a walk
  Down street today;
I saw lots of people
  Along the way.

Mr. Jones at his store
  Put out his head;
"Hi! Good morning!"
  Is what he said.

Old Mrs. Brown
  Was sweeping her walk,
And was not too busy
  To stand and talk.

A boy in a truck
  Waved his hand to me;
I don't know his name
  Or who he can be.

George the shoeman
  Fixes shoes;
He has to remember
  Whose is whose.

The man at the newsstand
  Said not a word;
And there in the gutter
  Was a poor dead bird.

BAD BOY

Lee Roy, he bad boy.
He been in jail;
He steals,
He takes things,
He a tattle tale.

He holler in the street,
He hurt a little kid;
He always start a fight,
He knocked me down, he did!

Better watch out,
Lee Roy, he mean;
He a bad boy—
Worst ever seen.

JOHNNY, COME HOME

Johnny, come home,
It's time to eat;
    I'll come in a minute,
    It's fun on the street.

Johnny, come home,
It's time for bed;
    No, I'm not sleepy,
    Can't hear what you said.

Johnny, come home,
Your bedtime's past;
    I'll stay up as long
    As the nighttime last.

Johnny, come home,
If you want to eat;
    No, you'll sure whip me—
    I'll sleep on the street!

79

HUNGRY

When the cupboard's empty,
    What we gonna eat?
Just a big ole soup-bone
    Without any meat?

Hey! My stomach's empty,
    Wisht I had a bean;
Find a few bread-crumbs,
    Lick 'em up clean.

When the cupboard's empty,
    How can we eat?
Golly, I'm hungry,
    Clear down to my feet!

SLUM HOME

Faucet's leaking,
    sink won't drain;
Somebody broke
    the windowpane.
Stuff a rag in
    to keep out the rain.

No heat in the pipes,
    the roaches play,
Chair's broke down,
    it rains all day.
Where's my Mom?
    she's gone away.

Cupboard's empty,
    kitchen's bare,
Nothing to eat
    anywhere;
Clothes on the floor—
    does nobody care?

Poor old sofa
    has seen its best day;
Go call the junkman,
    haul it away;
Take all the furniture—
    don't stop to pay.

Neighbors are noisy,
    scream and yell;
Somebody get hurt?
    are they sick or well?
If they're in trouble,
    you never can tell.

I SAT ON THE STOOP

I sat on the stoop
      and the wind blew cold,
Pulled sweater up as tight
      as I could hold;
Watched all the people,
      strange people go by,
No one stopped to look
      or notice how I cry.

I sat on the stoop
      and nobody knew
How lonely I was
      as the cold wind blew;
I sat on the stoop
      in the noise and the clatter,
Nobody asked me,
      What is the matter?

I sat on the stoop,
      alone, afraid,
Through all the noise
      the children made;
I sat on the stoop
      as they played nearby,
But nobody said,
      You don't need to cry.

Nobody said,
      Don't cry today,
Tomorrow will be better,
      Wipe the tears away;
Nobody gave me
      a word of cheer,
Nobody said,
      I love you, dear.

ALL THE PEOPLE ON OUR STREET

All the people on our street
Are people that I like to meet.

I take a walk and say hello
To all the people that I know.

Some are happy, some are gay;
Some just look the other way.

Some are cross and look so sad,
As if a friend they never had.

Some go walking very fast,
Going somewhere, rushing past.

Some are deaf and never hear,
Even when I'm standing near.

Then there are those I like the best,
For they are different from the rest.

They stop their work and turn to see
Who is talking—
                    and it's ME!

LONESOME PLACE

The city is a lonesome place,
    Though filled with people gay;
It sometimes offers pleasure,
    But chases friends away.

The city is a lonesome place,
    It bangs and knocks and hums;
It never offers quiet,
    Or peace that softly comes.

Your nearest city neighbor
    Will never speak to you;
To him you are a stranger—
    He is a stranger too.

The city has forgotten
    Or never knew your name;
It offers only blarney,
    And never mentions fame.

The city is a lonesome place,
    Full of unknown fears;
It sends dark shadows to a room,
    And fills up eyes with tears.

TIME

Give me a nickel,
Give me a dime;
Mama, I want to
     have a good time.

Child, I got no nickel,
Child, I got no dime;
Got to keep on payin'
   for things on time.

TV's not paid for,
So much a week;
Radio's broken,
Gives only a squeak.
Wash machine's owing,
Dryer too;
Insurance man's coming,
Payments overdue.

When I reach in my purse, child,
There's nothing there,
But heat and light bills
   and empty air!

Without a nickel,
Without a dime,
Mama, how can I
     have a good time?

YOU ALWAYS HAVE TO PAY

Everything costs money,
No matter what you buy;
Everything has to be paid for—
Don't pass the cashier by.

Everything costs money,
No matter where you go;
In store or bank or subway,
In theater or movie show.

Everything costs money,
No matter what you do;
Eating, drinking, playing
Or buying clothes so new.

Everything costs money,
Nothing is free today;
So save your dimes and pennies—
You always have to pay.

But you don't need money for kindness,
For sunshine, the clouds or the breeze;
The love or the smile of your mother—
You don't have to pay for these.

MY PURSE IS FULL OF MONEY

My purse is full of money,
A twenty dollar bill;
I'm going to the store
All my wants to fill.
I'll take along my money
And I'll buy out the store;
I'll come back again
And buy a lot more.

I'll buy me a doll,
    A doll that can walk—
The kind that says Mama,
    Can laugh, cry and talk.

I'll buy pearls and rubies,
    Diamond ring for a dime;
Bracelets and earrings
    And a watch that keeps time.

I'll buy me a wedding dress
    That has a long train;
A veil to hang down
    And make me feel vain.

I'll buy a live pony,
    On its back I can ride;
I'll sit on the saddle,
    My whip at my side.

My purse is full of money,
I'll buy out the store;
I'll come back again
And buy a lot more.

LAY-AWAY

On a hot July day
  We went downtown,
To buy my winter coat
  And pay something down.

We knew all about
  The lay-away plan;
We'll pay each week
  As much as we can.

It will be all paid for
  By Christmastime;
Before cold weather,
  The coat will be mine.

We'll go down and get it
  On a very cold day;
I'll put it on and wear it
  And run out to play.

LONG LIFE

Old Grandpa Fishbein
    was a hundred years old today;
All his children and his friends
    came for a party gay.

All day long
    he sat in his easy chair,
    as the people came and went;
Birthday cake and cold turkey
                for all—
    and he was quite content.

Old Grandpa Fishbein
    got tired of shaking hands,
    leaned back and slept awhile;
The people on our block
    brought a big bouquet,
He opened his eyes
    and gave them a smile.

A telegram came from the Mayor,
    and one from the Governor too;
Eat well, don't smoke or tell a lie,
          said Grandpa;
    and a very long life to you!

LITTER

Litter in the gutter
        all along the street,
Furniture abandoned,
        beds with springs complete;
Papers, kitchen garbage
        thrown out anywhere,
Empty boxes, rubbish,
        bottles here and there.

Litter in the gutter,
        on all the streets about;
Where did it ever come from—
        someone threw it out.
Let us stage a clean-up,
        clear it all away,
And then we'll all hope
        that clean it will stay.

CLEANING UP THE BLOCK

Bring your shovel,
Bring your broom,
We're cleaning up the block.
Get a spade
Come and help—
We're cleaning up the block.

Get rid of the trash,
Get rid of the rats,
Broken bottles and empty cans;
Old waste paper and boxes,
Broken toys and frying pans.

Dump the rubbish in the truck
And haul it far away;
We are cleaning up the block,
And clean it's going to stay.

REHABILITATION

They tore our house down,
  We have to get out;
They gave us no time
  To look about.

They say they will find us
  A place to live;
Nothing but promises—
  That's all they give.

Rehabilitation they call it—
  To send us away
From the block we love,
  Where we want to stay.

We have to get out
  Leave the place we know,
Get out and live somewhere—
  But where can we go?

URBAN RENEWAL

Tear down the old
  And build up the new;
Let fall the wall,
  The rooftop too.

Old shabby slum
  For a new high-rise,
Twelve stories up
  To touch the skies.

Build up with steel,
  Concrete and stone,
Displacing the people—
  And the wrong condone.

Urban renewal,
  A city made new;
How soon will all this
  Be outdated too?

MY HOME IN THE CITY

CITY CHILD

The sidewalk is my yard,
  The lamppost is my tree;
Up three long flights of stairs,
  My home is Flat 4C.

The fire escape my porch,
  Where clothes hang out to dry;
All day the noise and rush,
  At night the trains go by.

Tall buildings all around
  Reach up and shadow me;
Sometimes the great big sun
  Comes peeping round to see.

All day the people pass,
  They hurry as they go;
But when they are my friends,
  They stop and say hello.

HOME IN THE SKY

Twelve stories high,
My home in the sky;
Out the windows a view
    Of the city too.

Twelve flights of stairs
All the way to the top;
The elevator takes us
    Where we want to stop.

All kinds of people
Live on our floor;
When some move out,
    In come some more.

All kinds of people
For neighbors have we;
Some cross and unfriendly,
    Some nice as can be.

Neighbors on top of us,
Under us too;
Neighbors beside us
    Who hear all we do.

High-rise apartment,
My home in the sky;
I look out the window—
    And wish I could fly!

BOY DOWN THE HALL

Who is the boy down the hall?
    Why doesn't he speak to me?
Why doesn't he tell me his name,
    So I can tell him about me?

Who is the boy down the hall?
    He never says a word to me;
Sometimes I wonder if he knows
    How lonely I can be.

Who is the boy down the hall?
    He looks very lonely and sad;
If he'd only talk, we'd be friends,
    And both of us then could be glad.

DREAM DOG

My dog is big and his name is Rocky,
He wags his tail and acts very cocky;
He lies at my feet—his favorite place—
He climbs up on me to lick my face.

I throw a stick and he brings it back,
I don't let him run on the railroad track;
I buy dog food, give him bones to chew,
He stays beside me whatever I do.

My dog is a watchdog, night and day,
He barks very loud, keeps the robbers away;
He bites the mailman who comes to the door,
He bites the policeman and makes him sore.

Rocky's my dog, my dream-dog pet,
No other dog can compare with him yet;
The other kids can't have pets, you see—
But they can't take Rocky away from me!

HIGH-RISE PROJECT

High-rise project,
   Low-cost price;
Twelve flights up—
   Elevator's nice.

Go spend a nickel,
   Go swipe a dime;
Put you in jail
   Your whole lifetime.

High-rise project,
   Low-cost purse;
Come dance a jig—
   It can't get worse!

I LIVE UPSTAIRS

I live upstairs
    On the very top floor;
We have a buzzer
    To open the door.

From apartment ten
    I look down on the street;
The people are walking
    Beneath my feet.

When I am down
    I climb up, and then
I wish I was
    Back down again!

CLOTHESLINE

Out on the fire escape
To hang out the clothes;
A squeak of the pulley
As the soft wind blows.

A tug on the rope
The clothesline brings;
Then over the courtyard
The clothesline swings.

Snap on the clothes pins,
Pin the clothes tight;
Pants, shirts and dresses,
All colors bright.

Hard in the wind
The wet clothes fly;
Snap back and forth
Until they are dry.

OUR FLAT IS HOT

Our flat is hot
On a summer day;
In the park so cool
We go to play.

We sit on a bench
Enjoy the cool breeze;
We like to stay out
Under the trees.

SPARROWS

Cheep, cheep, cheep!
Sparrows chirping at my feet,
You want crumbs to eat?

Cheep, cheep, cheep!
Sparrows hop and jump and fight,
Try to get a bite.

Cheep, cheep, cheep!
Sparrows chirping, I'm like you,
I am hungry too.

Cheep, cheep, cheep!
Sparrows chirping, fly away,
I have no crumbs for you today.

MOM HAS A JOB

Mom has a job,
To work she goes;
She leaves the house
Before daylight shows.

Mom goes to work
And stays all day;
She has to earn money
Our bills to pay.

She has a hard job,
She sits and sews
At a power machine,
Making clothes.

Other women work
And sew there too;
Each day they are given
Many pieces to do.

The more they work,
The more they earn;
Mom can sew faster
The seams to turn.

Mom comes home late
And tired too;
I sit on her lap
When dinner is through.

FLOWER SO RED

Flower so red
In an earthen pot,
In the dark shadow,
It makes a bright spot.

Flower so red,
Stem so slight,
Reaching upward
Toward the light.

Outside the window
A splash of red,
Drying clothes
Flap overhead.

Flower so red
On the windowsill,
Bring joy and beauty
My heart to fill.

SMELLS

What do I smell—
Cabbage cooking?
Yes, I know it
Without looking.

Bacon frying—
Breakfast neat;
How many slices
Can I eat?

Two nice fried eggs,
Sunny side up;
Coffee enough
To fill a cup.

When you buy fish,
Oh, what a smell!
But when you eat it,
It sure tastes swell!

PIGEONS ON THE ROOFTOP

Pigeons on the rooftop,
    Pigeons fly away;
But always they come back
    The very same day.

A box for my pigeons,
    Grain for them to eat;
    Each one is beautiful
    With tiny pink feet.

Each one a messenger
    To some one far away,
Bringing grace and beauty
    To a dull day.

Pigeons on the rooftop—
    All day long they coo,
And even if they fly away
    Fly back to me too.

A LITTLE GREEN THING

I found a little green thing
    Growing in a crack;
I pulled it up so gently—
    I could not put it back.

It had some green leaves on it,
    And roots that hung below;
I found an empty beer can
    And dirt to make it grow.

I wanted it to make a bud,
    A pretty flower too;
I poured on lots of water—
    That's all that I could do.

It never made a flower,
    It never set a seed;
One day my mother threw it out—
    She said it was a weed.

MY DAD

My Dad is a big strong man,
He plays with me whenever he can;
He takes me to the candy store,
He wrestles with me on the floor.

He takes me to the ball games,
Where we stand up and shout;
He bought me bat and baseball—
I hit three strikes, I'm out!

My Dad makes lots of money,
Our bills he has to pay;
He wants to buy an auto,
And a house of our own some day.

HOME IN THE BASEMENT

Home in the basement
  Down the steps below,
The sun never shines
  And flowers never grow.

Lower than the sidewalk
  There are windows two;
When we pull the curtains,
  People can't see through.

Down in the basement
  With curtains open wide,
We watch the people's feet
  Go walking by outside.

It's dark and it's dingy,
  Damp and musty too;
You wish that it was better—
  That's all that you can do.

THE BEAR

A bear got loose from the city Zoo,
He came up the street and said,
                              "How do you do?"
I shook his paw and said with a smile,
"I'm fine—please stay and play awhile."

Said the big fuzzy bear,
Without ruffling a hair,
          "I'd like some bread,
          And I'd like some honey;
          But the trouble is,
          I have no money."

So I bought a honey sandwich fat,
And he gobbled it down just like that.
Then he turned so quickly and said, "good-bye,
Back to the Zoo I must surely fly.
          I want to go home, I do,
          I'm homesick for the Zoo."

I looked around—
          there was nothing there;
Up in thin air
          had vanished that bear!

TWO-ROOM FLAT

Up there at the window
I see her looking out;
I wave my hand
And give a big shout.

I climb in the darkness
The long stair flights;
To the topmost landing
With its dim lights.

A rap at the door,
I see a dear face;
And then I am lost
In my Mom's embrace.

The windows are broken,
The carpet torn;
Shabby the furniture,
Curtains forlorn.

Beloved two-room flat
For my Dad, Mom and me;
Shared only with cockroaches—
How happy are we!

OUR COURT

We live right next
To all our friends—
Five houses in a row;
In every house
A boy or girl—
We have not far to go.

We like our court,
It is the best—
We think of things to do;
We laugh and play,
We shout all day,
We fight and quarrel too.

But when bad times
And trouble come,
On neighbors we depend;
We like to help
Each other out—
We give and take and lend.

NO HEAT TODAY

Radiator's cold,
No heat today;
The room is clammy,
Mom's gone away.

Cold wind whistles
Through the window crack;
Beds unmade—
Mom's not back.

Open the cupboard,
A crust of bread;
Not much good,
But better than dead.

Mouse in the corner
Peeks round a shoe;
Give him a crumb—
He's hungry too.

STAR IN THE SKY

Ain't no trees,
Ain't no grass;
Nothing but streets
For traffic to pass.

Ain't no sunshine,
Most the time rain;
Big black shadows
On the windowpane.

Ain't no houses,
Just buildings tall;
Nothing but factories—
That is all.

Ain't no daylight,
Clothes won't dry;
But sometimes at night
A star in the sky.

NEVER A TREE

Never a tree to climb,
Never a brook to wade;
Never a swing to swing
Beneath a tree's cool shade.

Never the smell of a flower,
Never a bluejay bold;
Never a butterfly to catch
And all its wonder behold.

Never the joy of walking
Barefoot through the grass;
Never the fun of catching
Fireflies as they pass.

Never the child of the city
The good green earth will know;
Never a blade or a flower,
To plant it and watch it grow.

CHILDREN OF THE CITY

Children of the city
    From tenements look down;
Walk the streets and sidewalks
    All around the town.

Children of the mansions
    Strolling in the park;
Children of the tenement
    Play out after dark.

Children of the city,
    Black and brown and white;
Arms around each other
    In friendliness unite.

INDEX OF TITLES

The source of previously published poems is given after the titles. Poems not so identified are published here for the first time.

INDEX OF FIRST LINES

Please see *"Index of Titles,"* page 113, for the original source of previously published poems.